WOMEN'S FASHION ILLUST[RATION] TEMPLATES

MW00885458

10-Head Fashion Figures

This Fashion Sketchbook includes six different curvy templates with different poses in side view, front view, back view and three quarters, to provide you with a variety of options to sketch your designs. It features lightly drawn figure templates so you can easily draw over them, and bring your ideas to life.

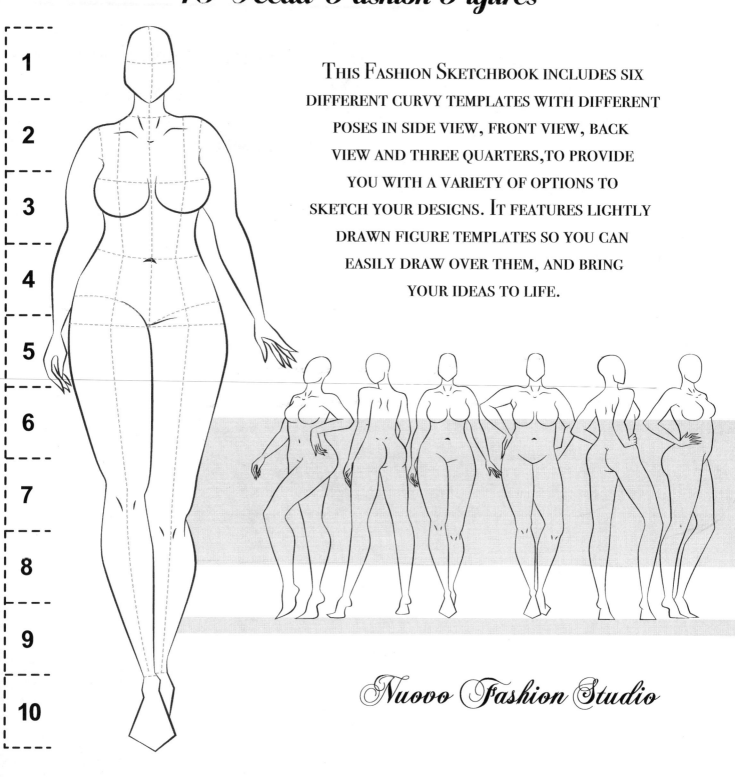

Nuovo Fashion Studio

Copyright © 2021 by Nuovo Fashion Studio. All Rights reserved

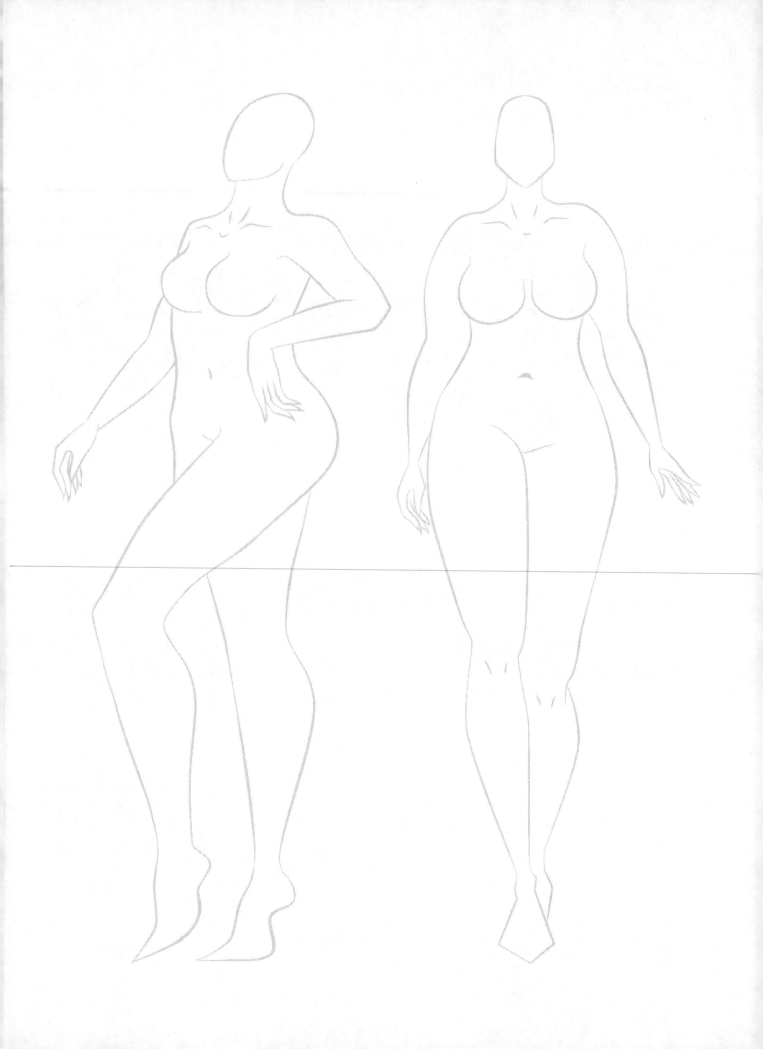

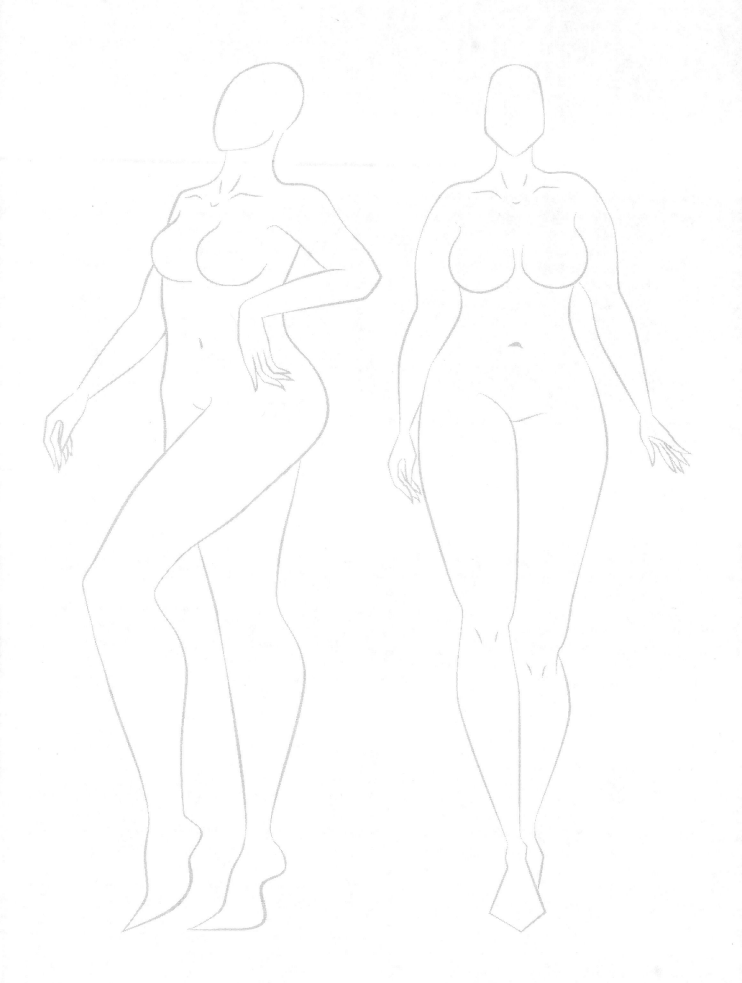

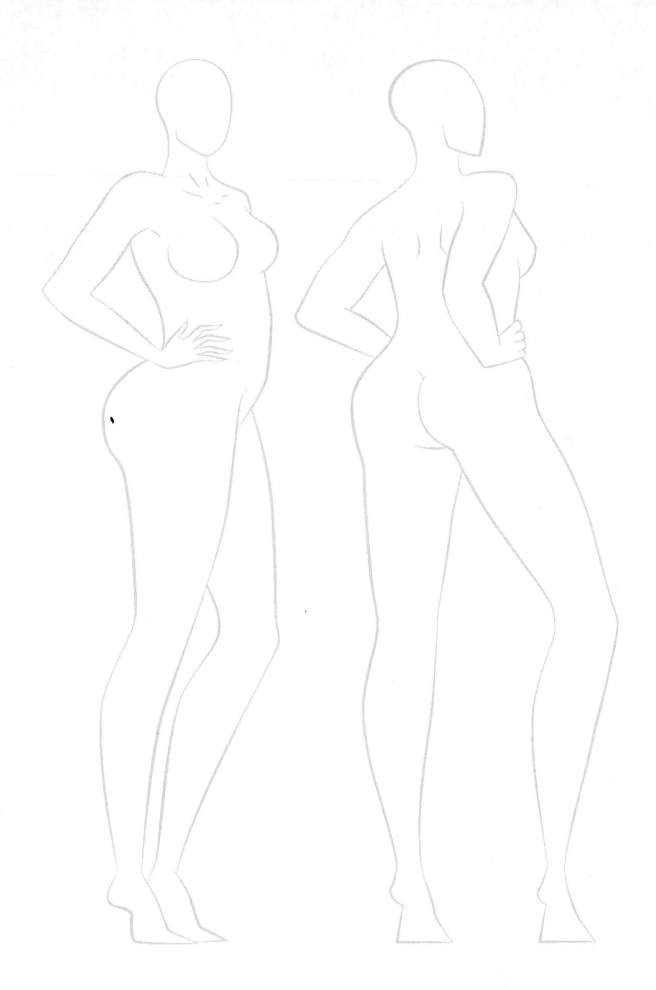

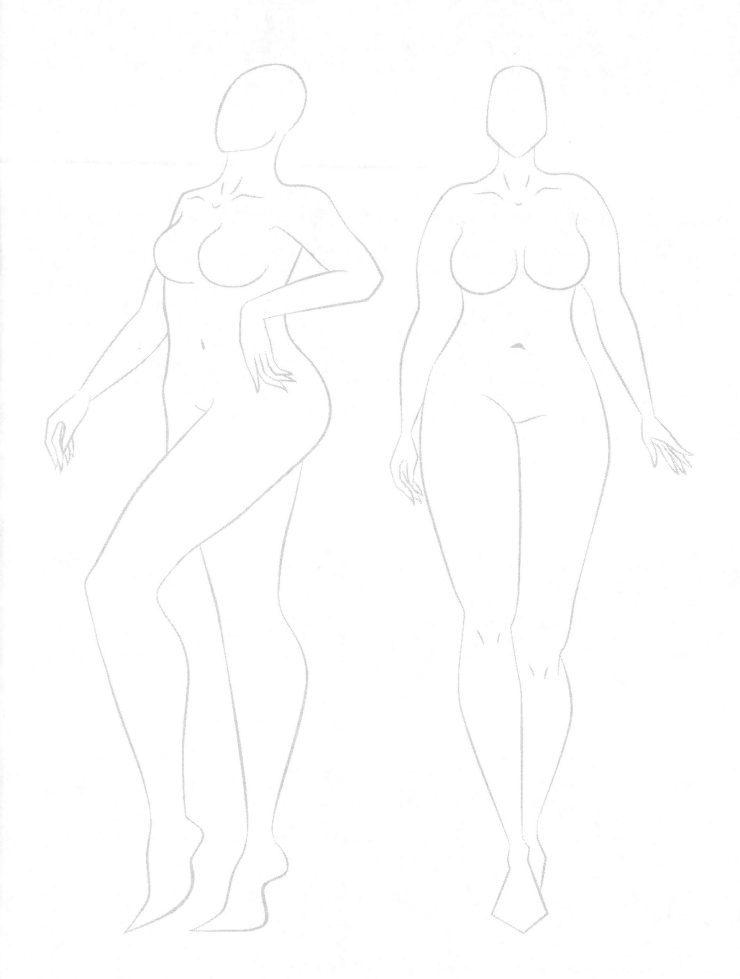

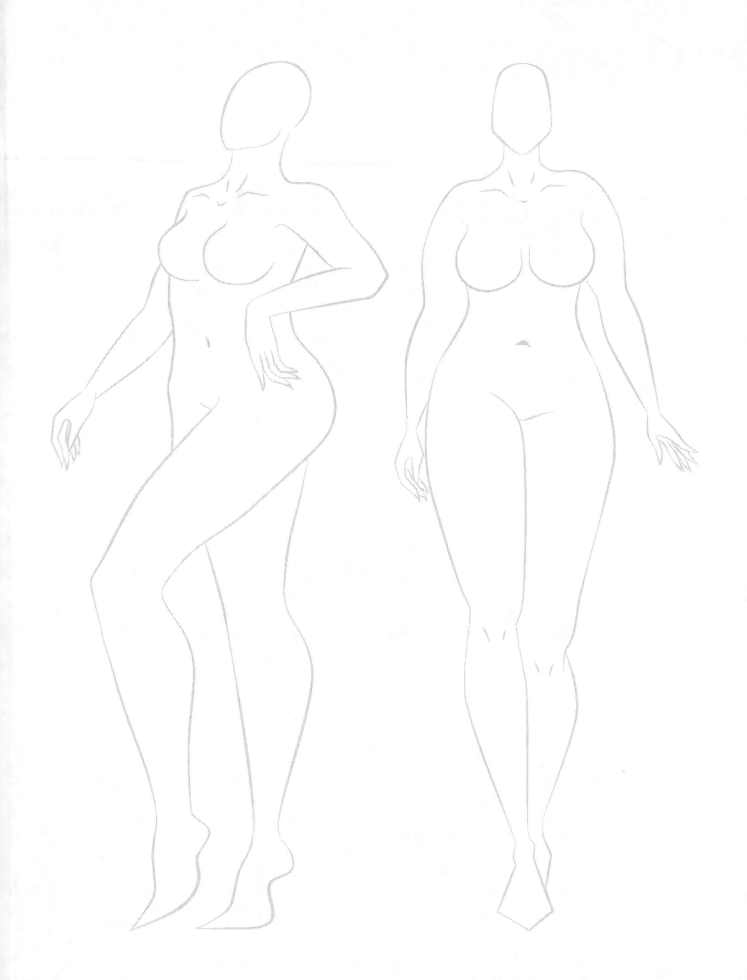

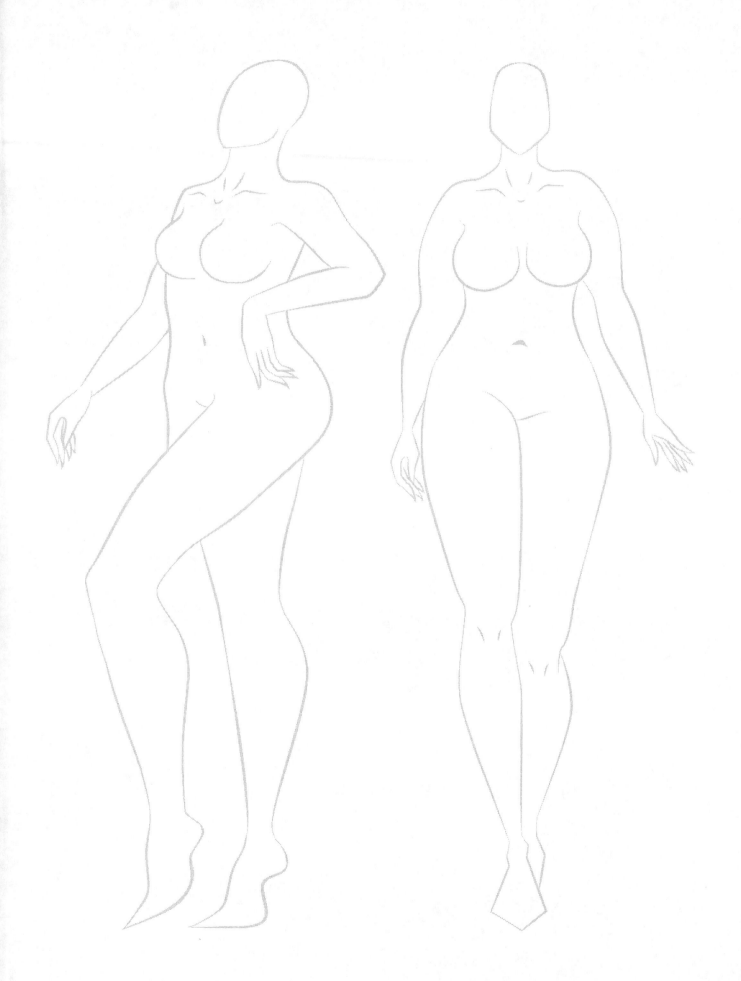

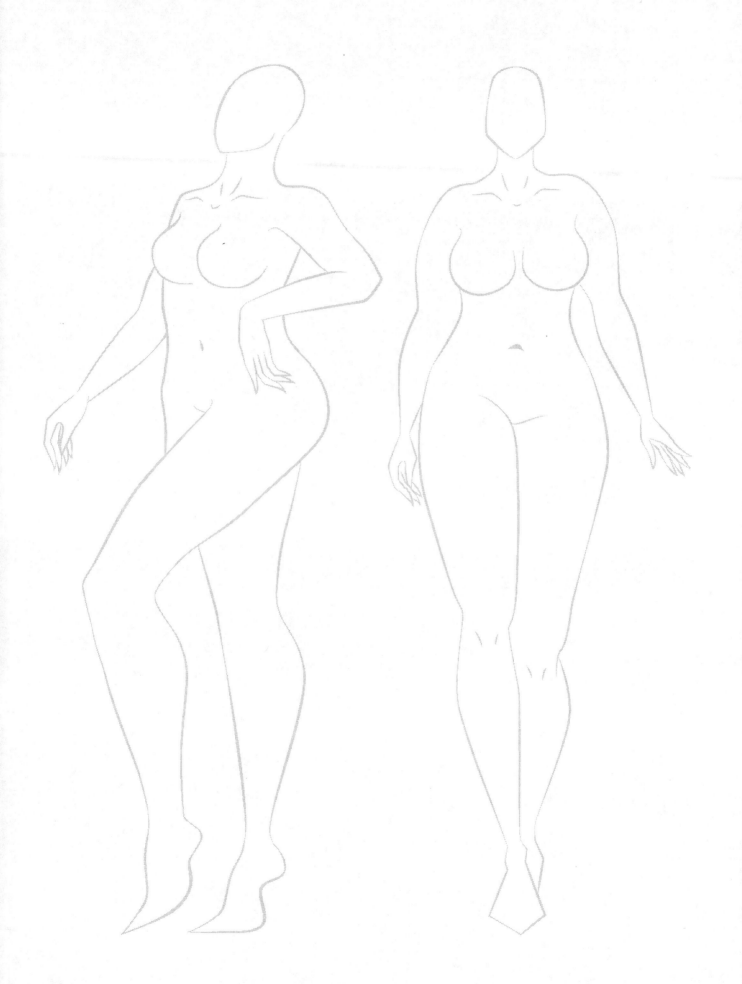

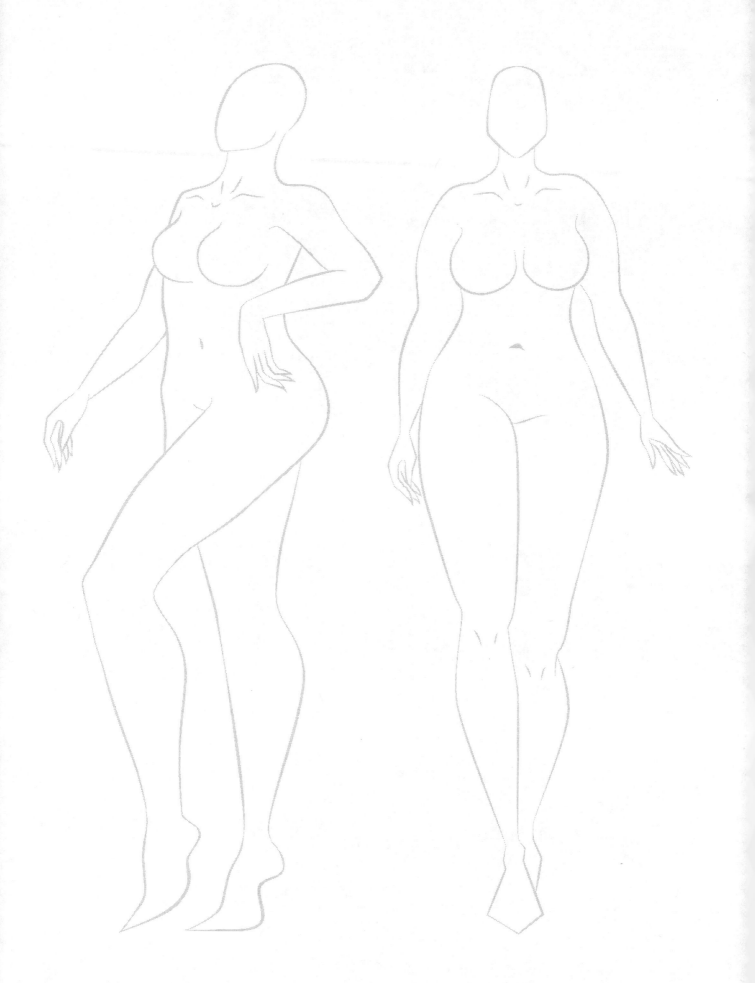

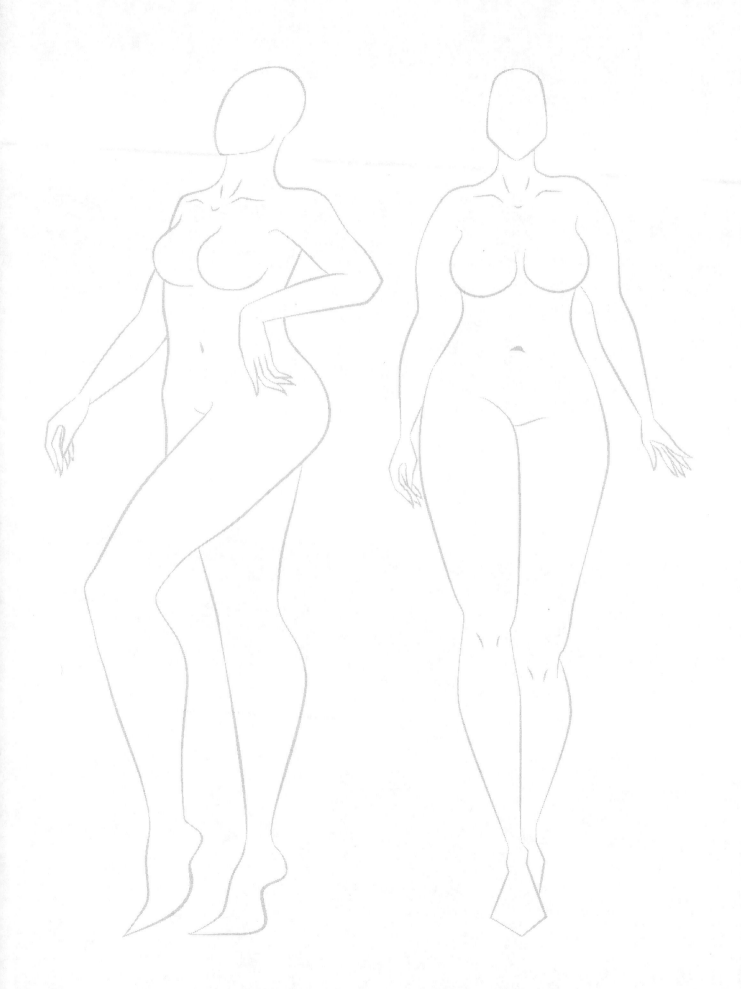

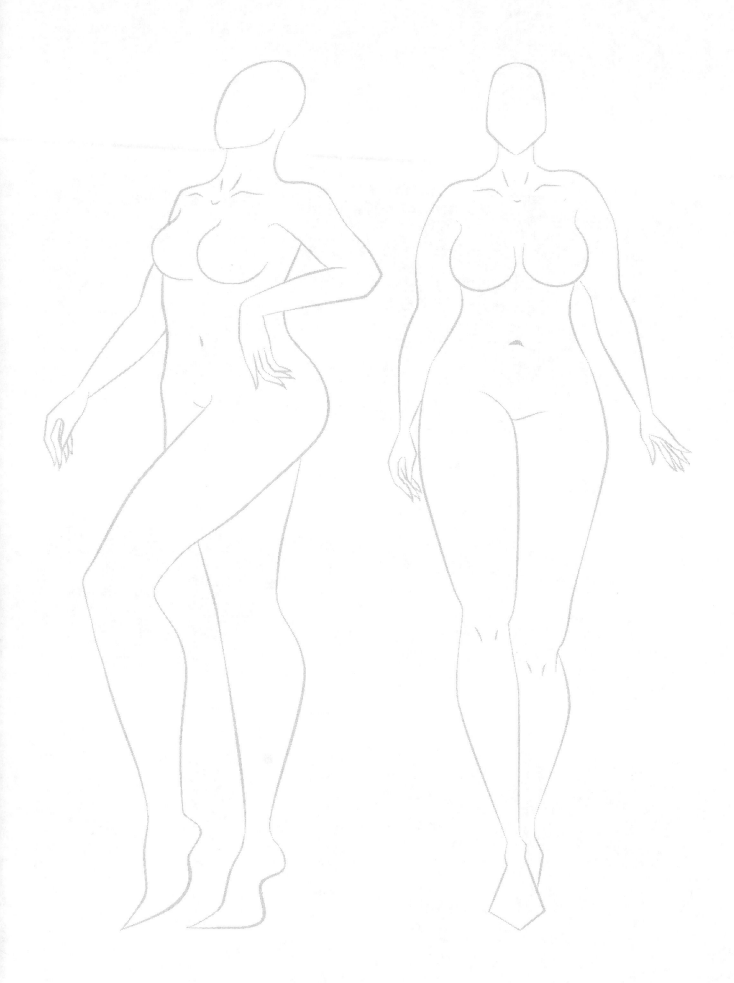

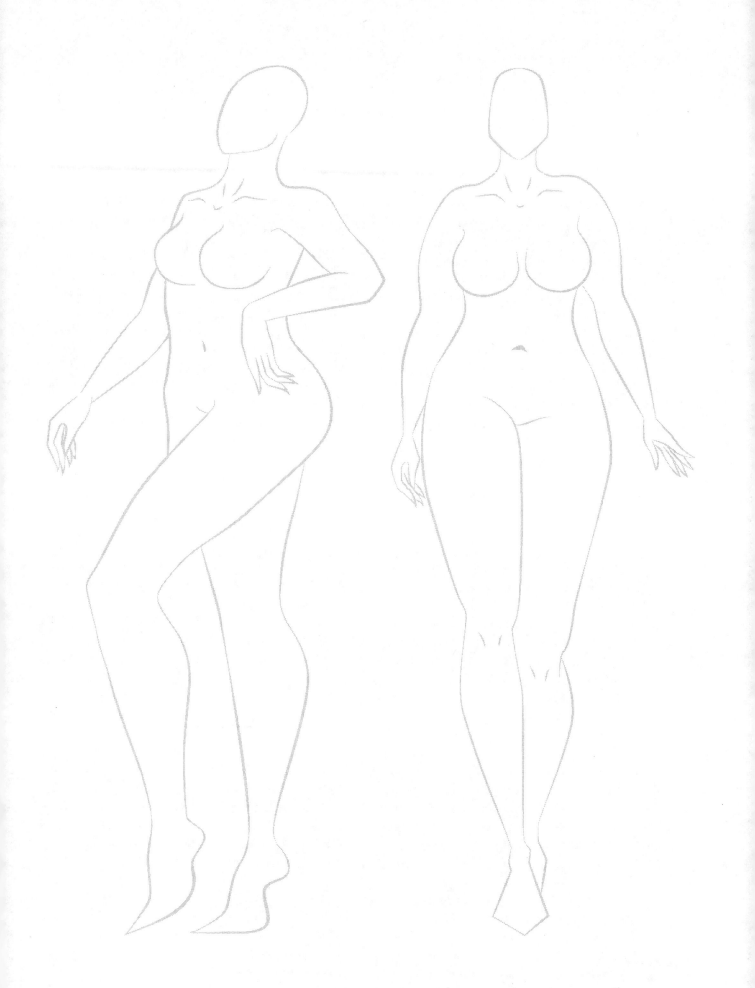

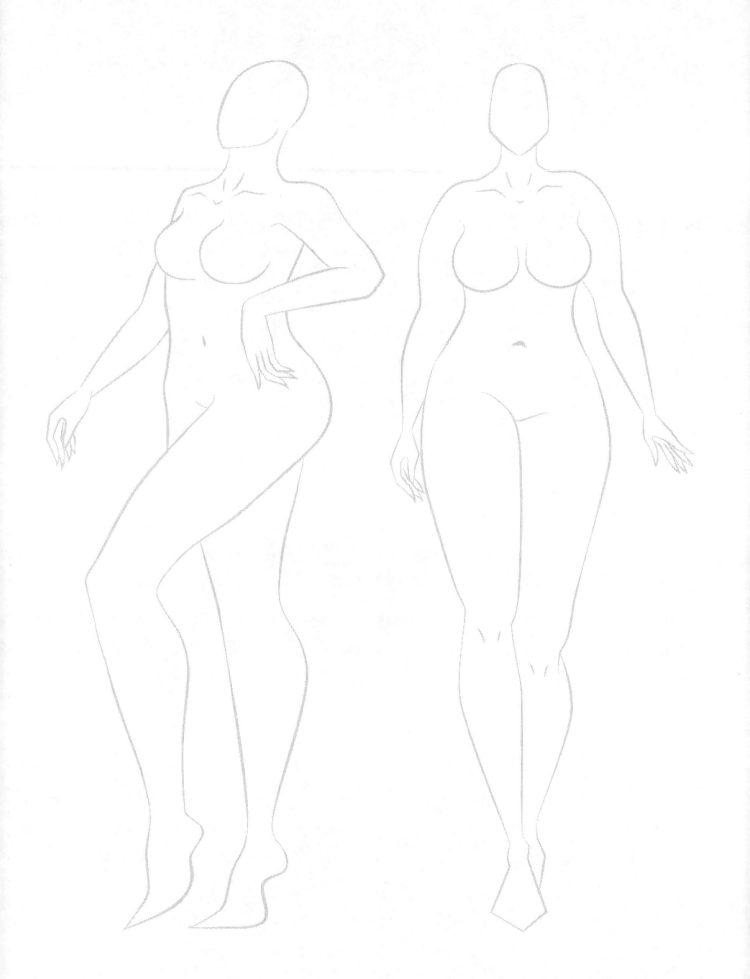

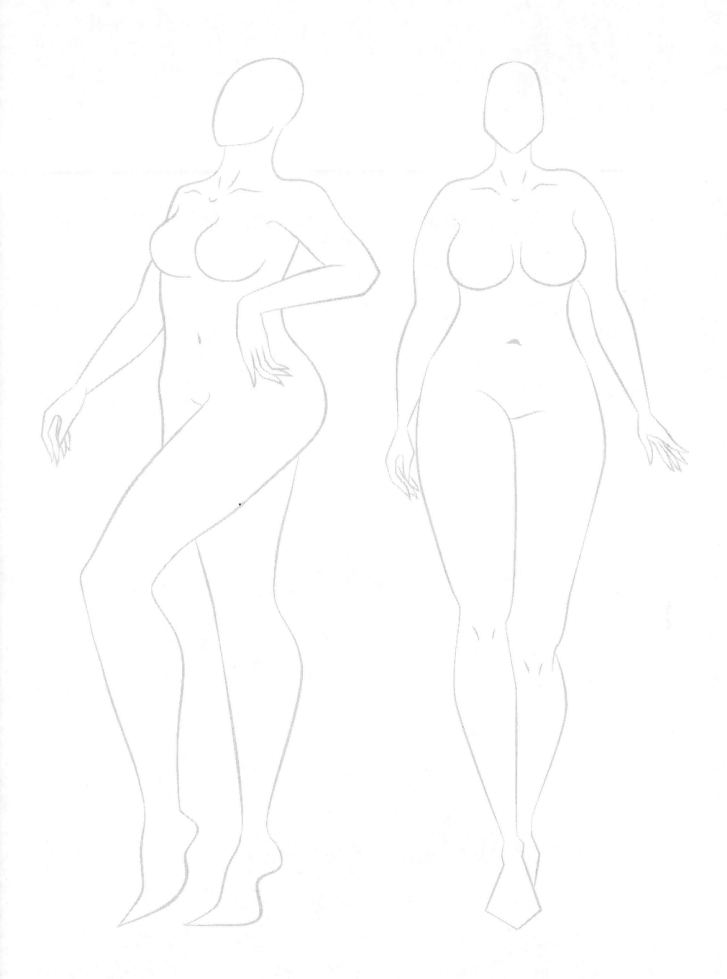

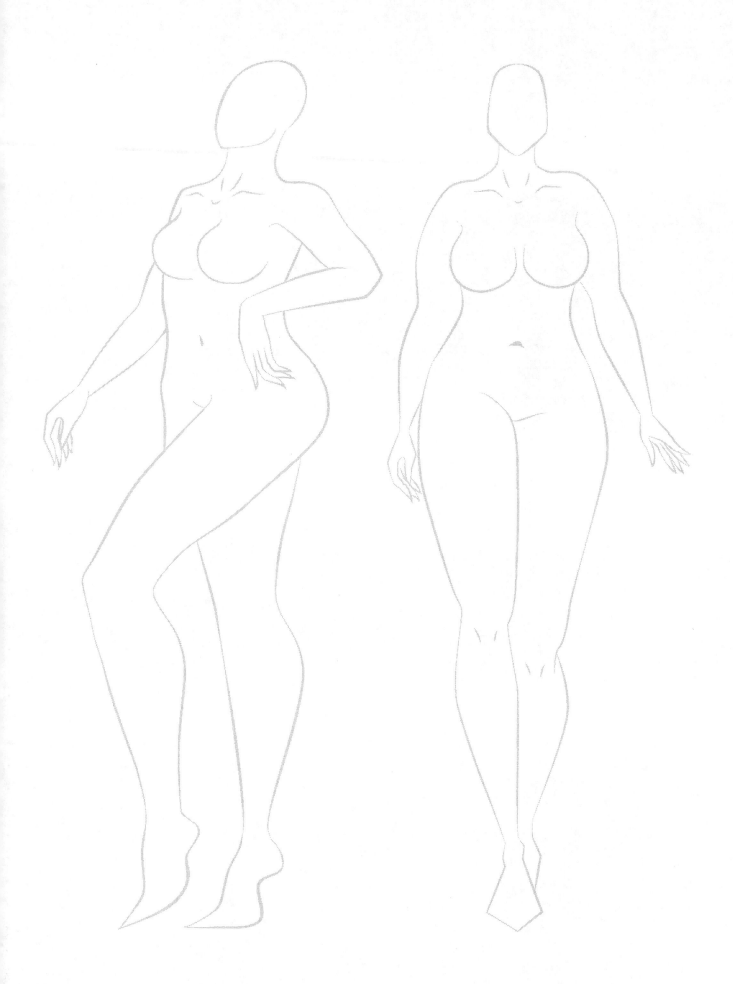

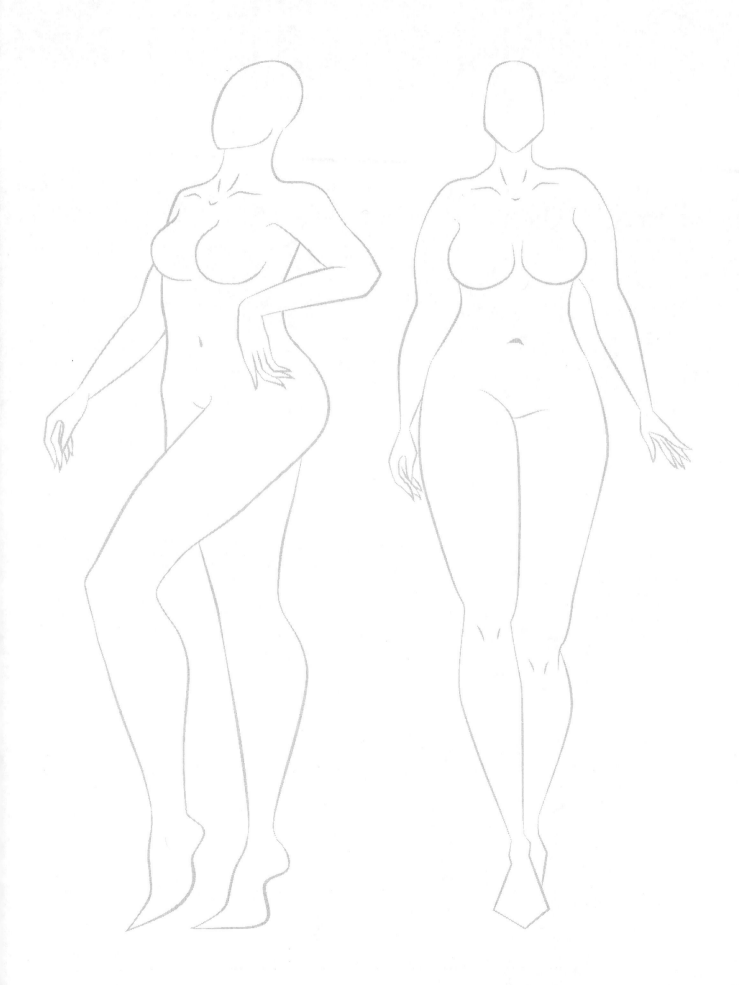

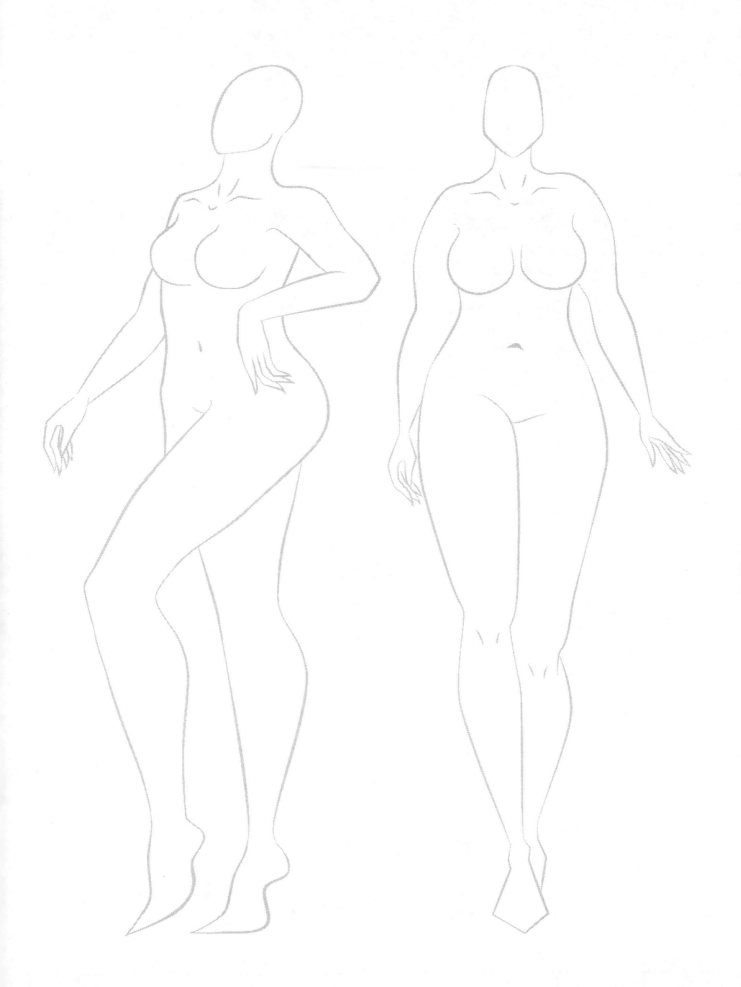

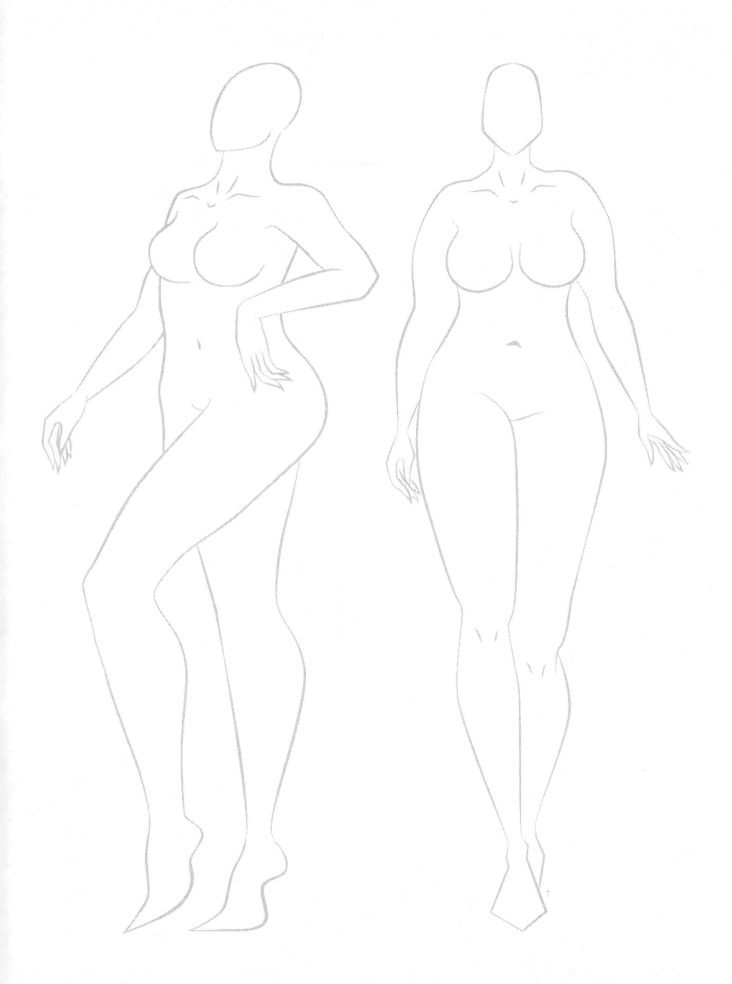

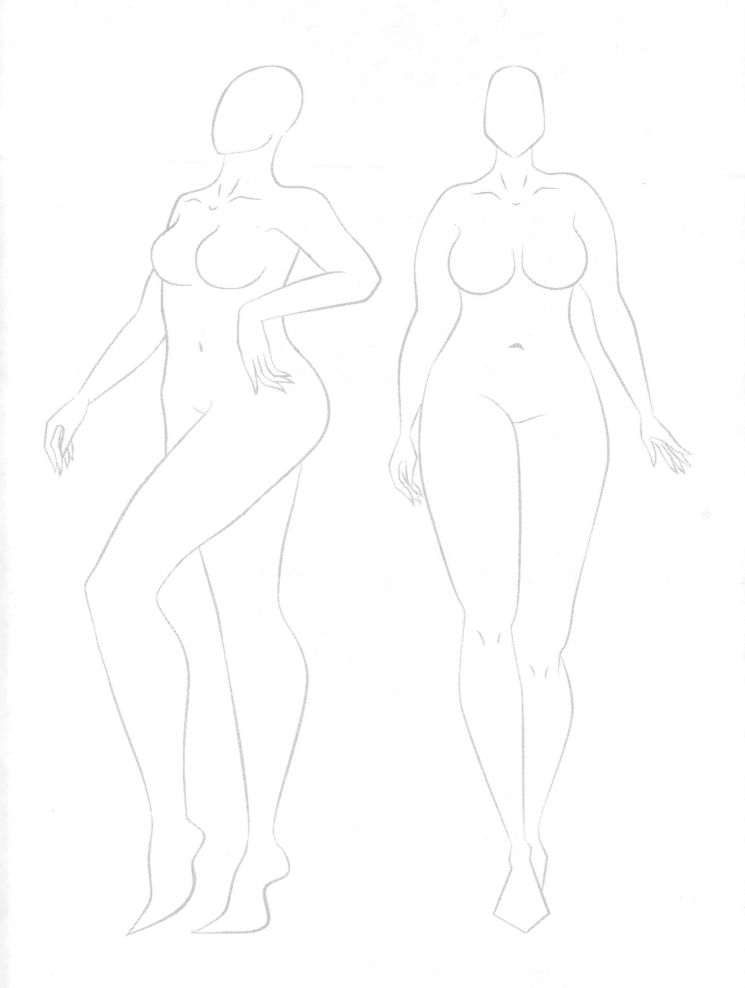

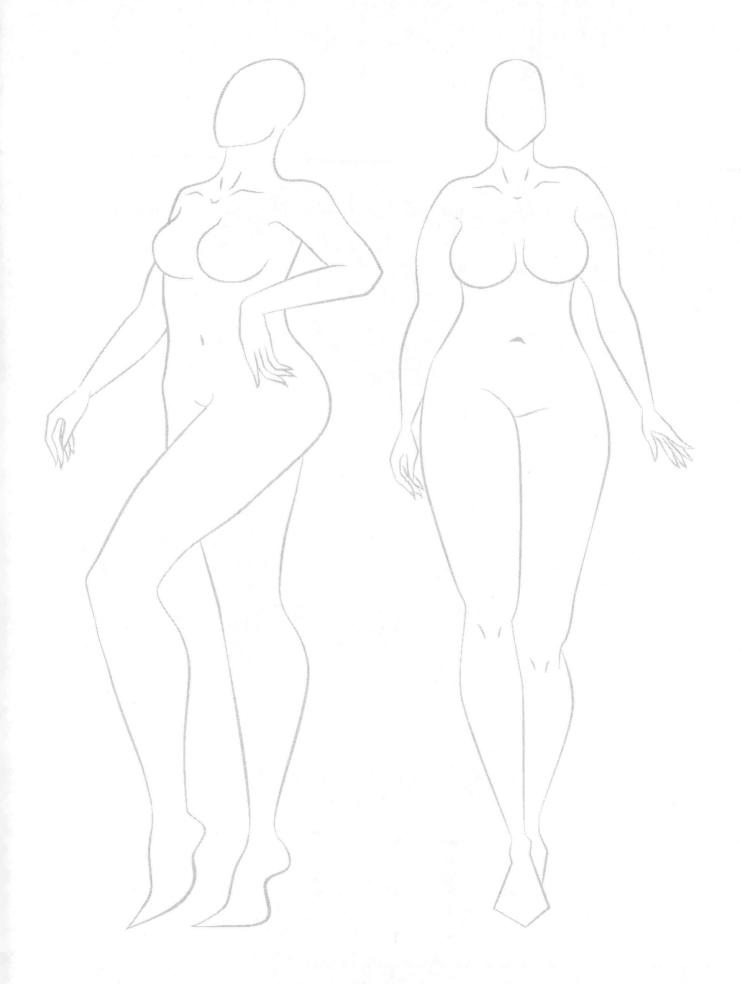

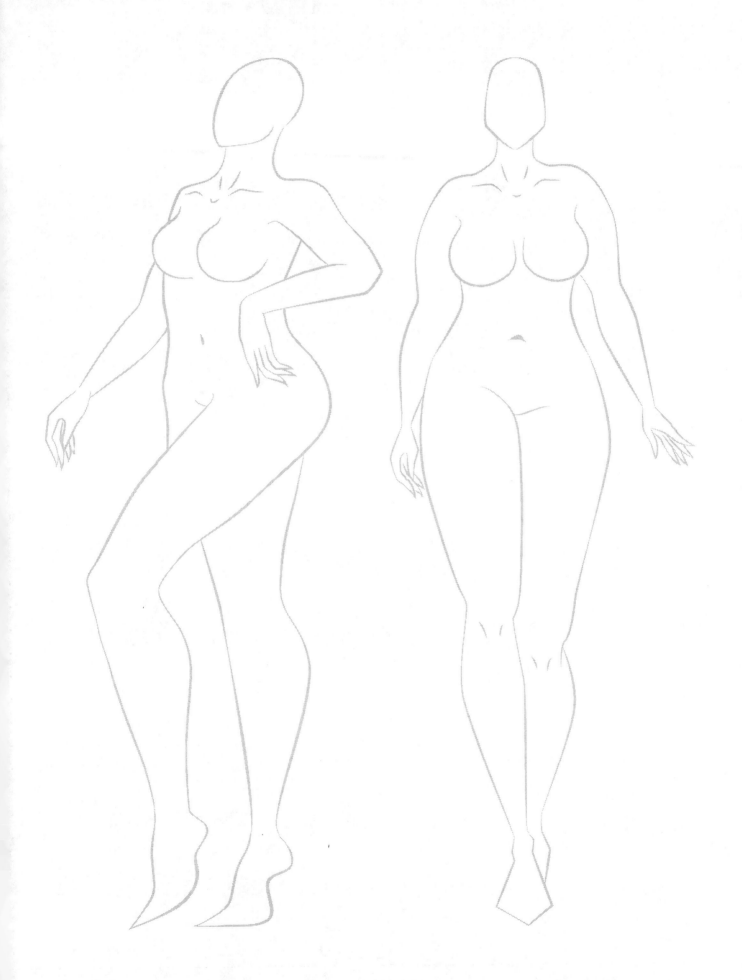

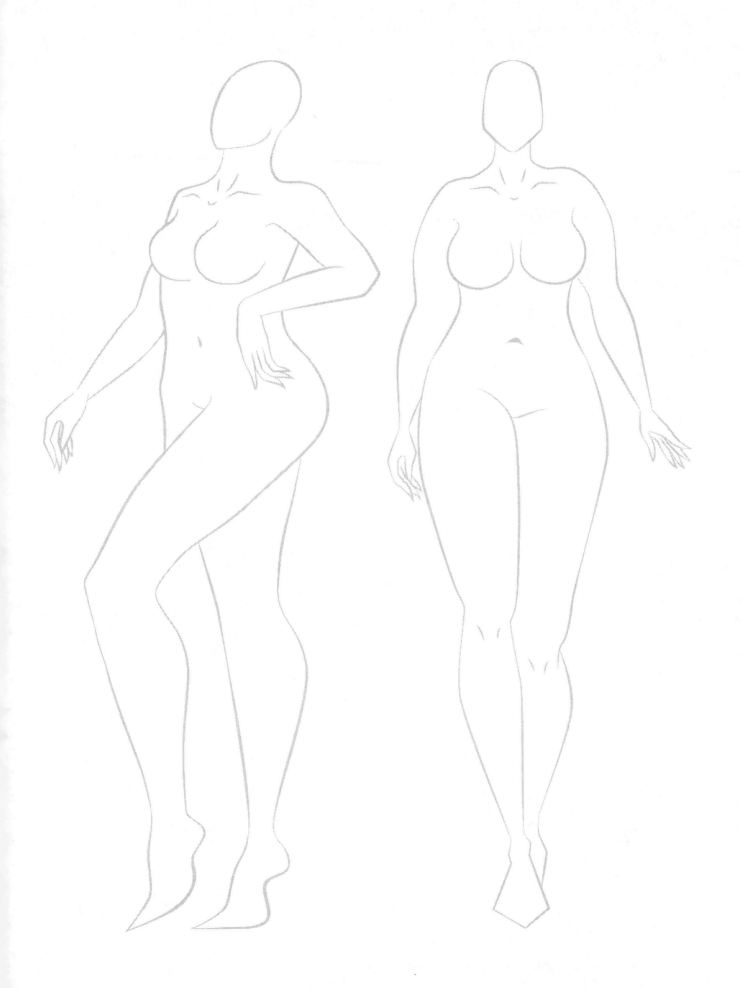

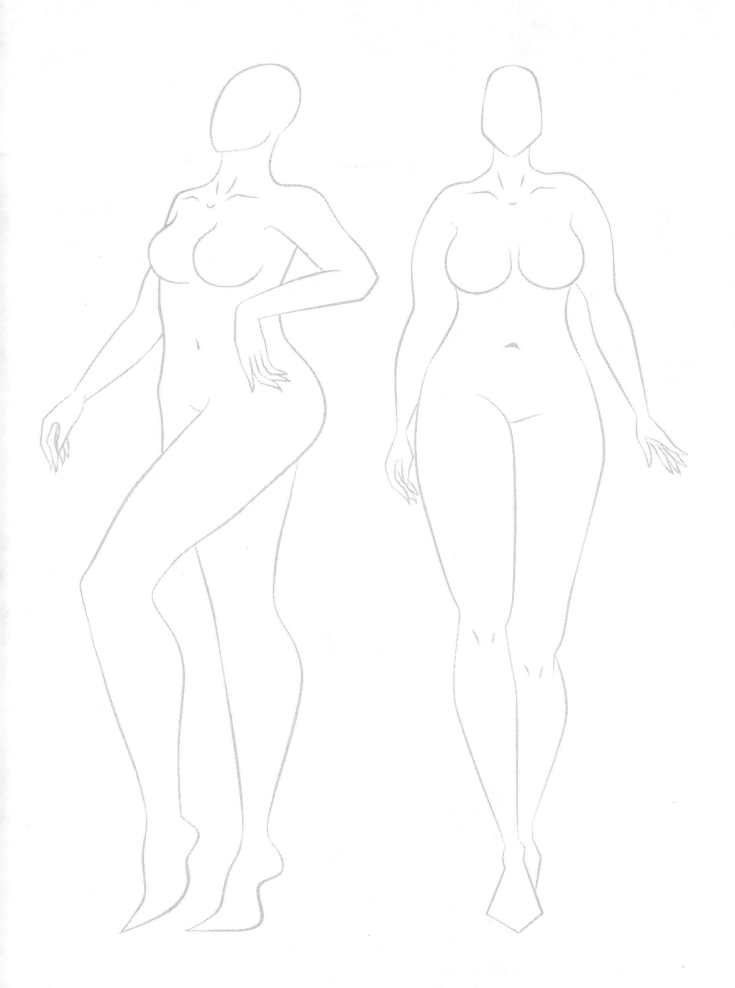

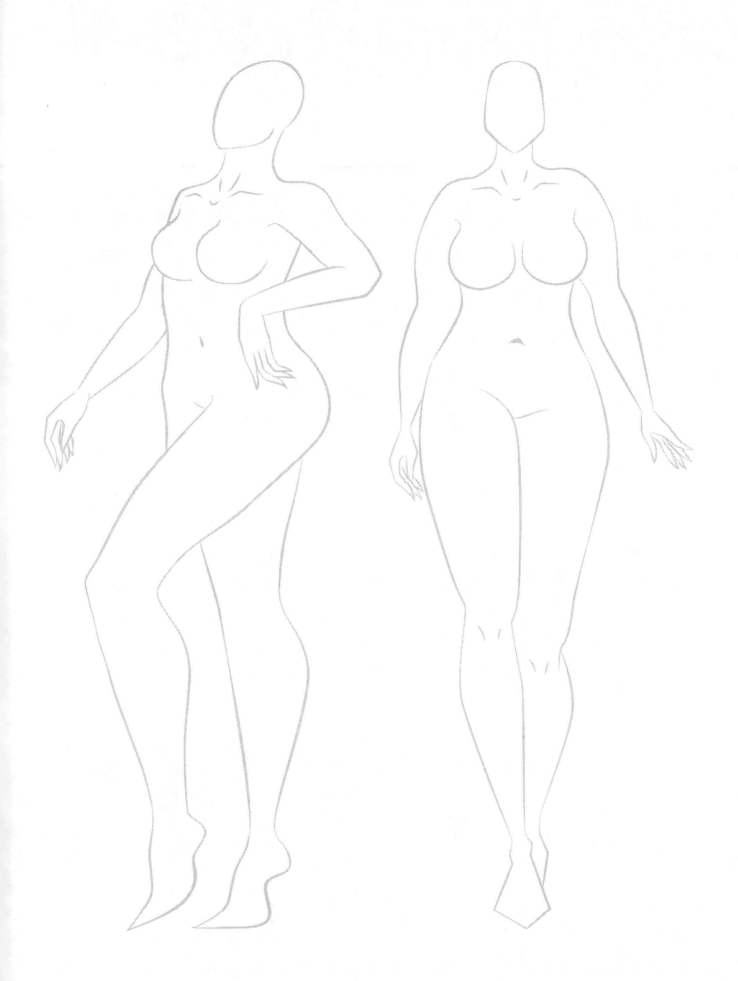

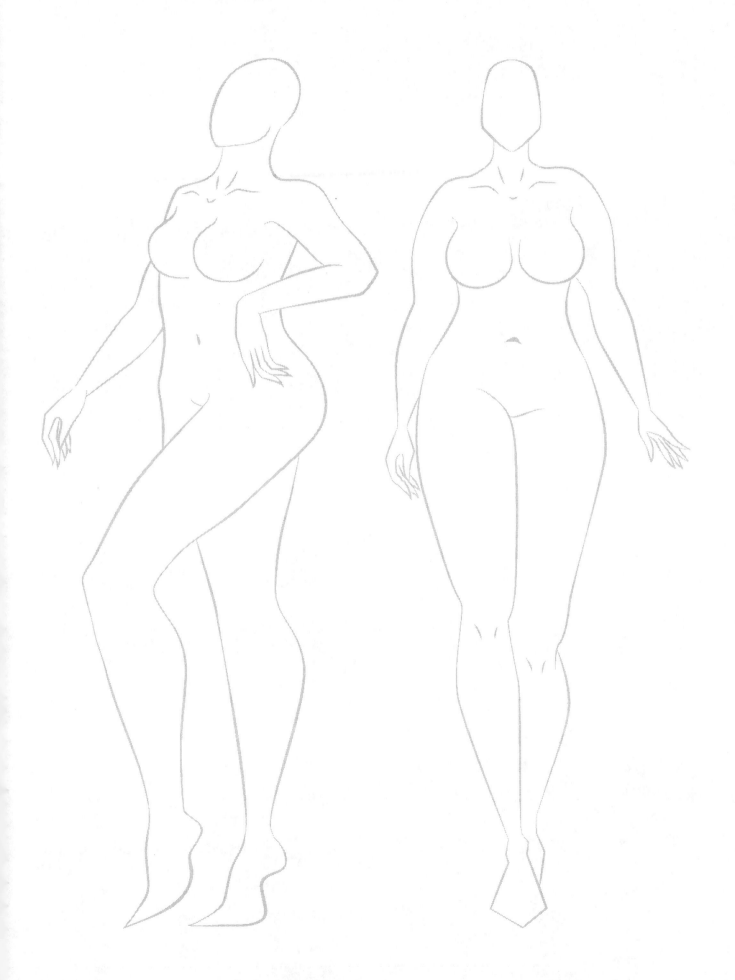

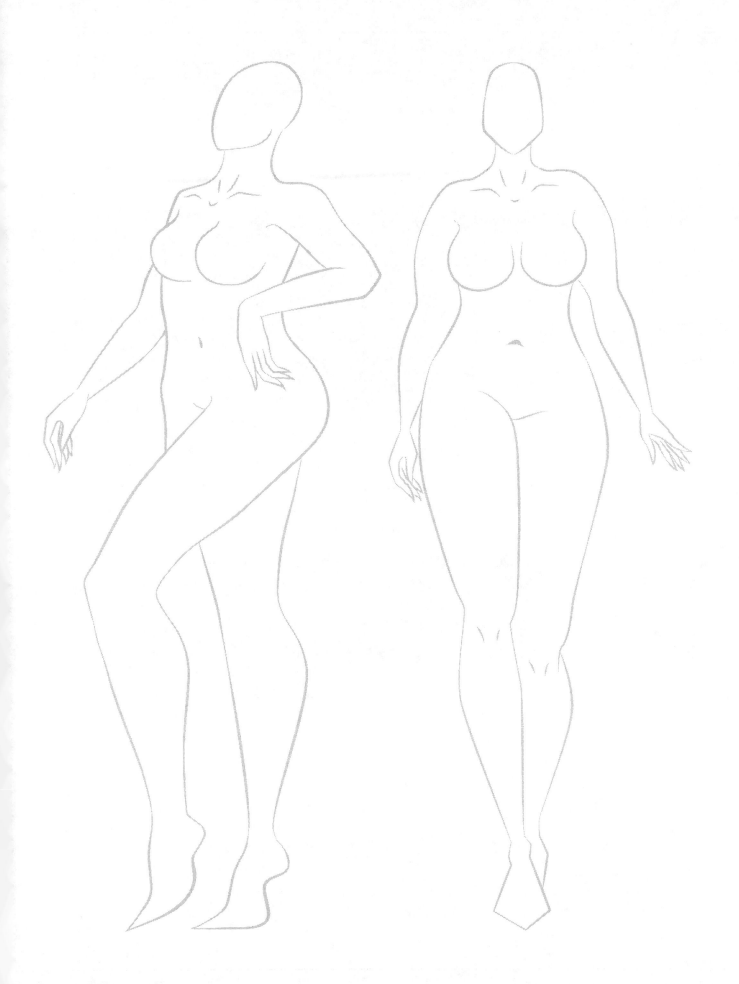

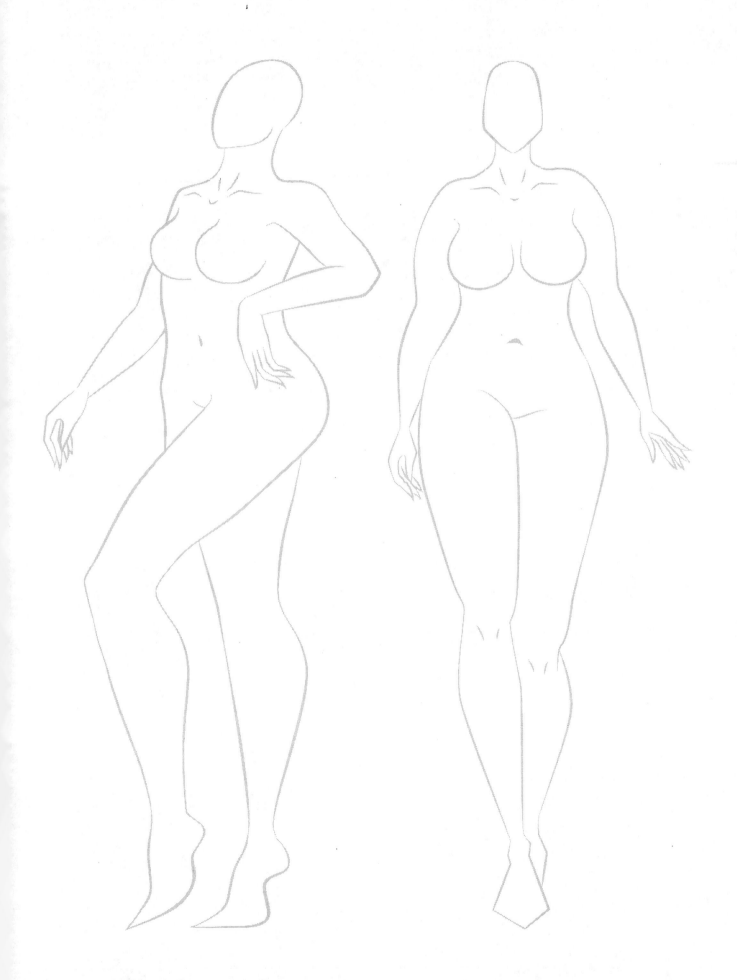

Made in the USA
Las Vegas, NV
22 December 2024

15227326R00085